Greater Works

Mandate For The Supernatural

Chad MacDonald

Revival Fire
PUBLICATIONS
www.miraclerevivalfire.com

Greater Works

Mandate For The Supernatural

Unless otherwise stated, all Scripture quotations are taken from the King James Version.

ISBN-13: 978-1725106642
ISBN-10: 1725106647
Copyright © 2018 by Chad MacDonald
Cover Design by John Polk
All Rights Reserved
Library of Congress Catalog Card Number: Pending
Printed in the United States of America

Table of Contents

Endorsements..11

Foreward..17

Chapter 1- Miracle Mandate........................23

Chapter 2- Endued With Power....................33

Chapter 3- The Kingdom of God..................49

Chapter 4- The Gifts of The Holy Spirit...........61

Chapter 5- Revelation Gifts........................73

Chapter 6- Vocal Gifts..............................81

Chapter 7- Power Gifts.............................89

Chapter 8- Partnering With The Holy Spirit.......97

Chapter 9- Walking in the Supernatural..........109

Conclusion...119

About The Author....................................127

Additional Resources.............................131

Endorsements

Evangelist Chad MacDonald's latest book, *Greater Works*, has personally challenged me and my ministry to be more of what Jesus has called me to be. This book points out exactly what is wrong with the modern day church as a whole, and the corrective steps needed for a course correction.

As believers we fall entirely too short of the power and authority that God has given us to walk in; *Greater Works*, is a rallying cry birthed out of the anointing that drives Chad. Chad simply cannot sit by and watch as untold numbers of souls remain under bondage of the enemy.

To effectively engage the enemy we must use our weapons of war, and this book is like a training manual that will get you battle ready.

Roger Randel, Pastor
Family of God Church
Topeka, KS

In *Greater Works,* Chad Macdonald sounds a clarion call to return to our spiritual DNA as believers. Citing that supernatural works are the norm for those who believe, he clearly outlines the essential person and purpose of the Holy Spirit. Whether you're a new believer or a seasoned disciple, this book will stir and remind you that it is only when we live in, by, and through the Spirit that both the world and the Church will know Jesus as He truly is!

Nathaniel Crane, Pastor
A Place of Meeting - Hope, Arkansas

Chad MacDonald's book, *Greater Works* is a call for all believers to rise up and fulfill the call of the Great Commission given to each of us by Jesus Christ. His passion to see people free from whatever may hold them captive or may be keeping them from being all that God has called them to be and do is a reflection of his love for the people he reaches.

This book is not for the easily offended. It is a book that will challenge believers to look beyond a shallow – "me" centered, Christianity to a desire to do the Greater Works that Jesus said we would do.

Cecy Zeis
Cecy Zeis Ministries

In his newest book, "Greater Works," Evangelist Chad MacDonald shares with us how our obedience to the Word of God and our submission to the Holy Spirit is in direct proportion to our ability to do the works of Jesus.

We will only see these miracles, healings and salvations as we yield ourselves to the Holy Spirit and realize that is has nothing to do with our ability and everything to do with His power working through us. This power does not come without a price either. We must live a sanctified life, we must fast and pray in the Holy Spirit and do whatever God tells us to do, even if it's not popular or pleasing to man. Evangelist MacDonald shares his passion to see the same miracles Jesus performed in His day performed on earth today! This book will stir you up to change how you are living, start praying everyday in the Holy Ghost and reach your world for Christ!

Rev. Don Zeis
Standard Bearer Ministries
Albuquerque, NM

Forward

Chad MacDonald has written another powerful book that will help equip and inform the Body of Christ. In 'Greater Works', you will discover or rediscover the necessity we have for the Holy Spirit. The unheard cry of our world today, is that they need an encounter with God. Not a manmade program but a touch from the creator himself.

We must have another great revival and awakening sweep across America and around the world. Many problems can be solved with the teachings found in this book filled and packed with the word of God.

'Greater Works' is a very timely book that had to be written. We so desperately need more books written about the Kingdom of God. This is a lost message to the church that has to be taught.

The world needs to hear the about the Kingdom and the power that is manifest when the Kingdom comes. Our Nation and world will be changed when we allow the Holy Spirit to have control of the church again.

I'm so thankful that Chad MacDonald isn't afraid to write about the error that is in the modern church.

'Greater Works' is a book that will encourage you to press into God for more. We must have the supernatural power of God working in our homes, families, churches and revivals.

We desperately need miracles to flow in every part of our life. God is looking for people to use in great measure these days. My good friend Chad MacDonald is one of these people.

Joe Joe Dawson, Apostle

ROAR Apostolic Network/ROAR Church

Texarkana, TX

Chapter 1
Miracle Mandate

"Verily, Verily, I say unto you, He that believeth on me, the works that I do shall he do also; and greater works than these shall he do; because I go unto my Father"
(John 14:12)

Regarding the ministry of Jesus, we see that everywhere He went, miracles seemed to follow. His ministry was indeed a ministry of the miraculous. It was one that was marked with power and demonstration. When Jesus showed up; dead things lived again, funeral processions came to a halt, blindness was wiped away, crippled limbs were made straight, leprosy vanished and demon power fled from His presence.

It is here in this fourteenth chapter of John that we discover these profound words...*'Greater works shall you do.'*
What a powerfully profound statement.
Could it even be possible? What was Jesus referring to?

Yet it seemed here that our Lord was giving a mandate to His disciples. It was in fact a mandate for the supernatural.
A mandate for miracles!

He was in fact telling His disciples that these very same works....

Miracles, Signs, Wonders

The very works you've seen.....mother's receiving their dead sons back to life again, withered hands being instantly restored, deaf ears popping open, cripples being made to walk again, the demon possessed being set free.
All these things and greater would they do.

Let's understand one thing. Jesus was referring to greater, not in quality but in quantity.

In the books of 1 and 2 Kings we find the narrative of the lives of the prophets Elijah and Elisha. Elijah being an Old Testament type and shadow of Christ and Elisha a type and shadow of the church.

It was Elisha that sought the double portion of Elijahs spirit and earnestly sought the mantle of Elijah.

"And it came to pass, when they were gone over, that Elijah said unto Elisha, Ask what I shall do for thee, before I be taken away from thee. And Elisha said, I pray thee, let a double portion of thy spirit be upon me. And he said, Thou hast asked a hard thing: nevertheless, if thou see me when I am taken from thee, it shall be so unto thee; but if not, it shall not be so." (2 Kings 2:9,10)

As Elijah was taken up into heaven, it was his protege Elisha who took up his mantle and continued his prophetic ministry. Elisha did indeed receive a double portion of Elijah's anointing. In fact Elisha performed exactly twice as many miracles as did Elijah.

In this you see an allude to what Jesus was saying in John 14. Here, in this text of scripture we find our Lord preparing his disciples for his impending departure.

In just a few days, Jesus would soon be crucified, resurrected from the dead and then subsequently ascend up into heaven to sit at the right hand of The Father clothed with power and glory.

However, Jesus tells His disciples that although He was about to leave them He would not leave them comfortless.

"And I will pray the Father, and he shall give you another Comforter, that he may abide with you for ever; Even the Spirit of truth; whom the world cannot receive, because it

seeth him not, neither knoweth him: but ye know him; for he dwelleth with you, and shall be in you. I will not leave you comfortless: I will come to you."

(John 14:16-18)

Jesus promised to send the Holy Spirit in His place and this blessed Comforter would not only be with us but would be in us.
Jesus said "I will come to you"
It is through the infilling of The Holy Ghost that we are enabled and empowered to fulfill the mandate of God for greater works.
Greater because, while Jesus was on the earth it was only he who operated through this manifestation of Holy Ghost power. Now, He was giving a resounding tag team handoff to all who believe in His name and would receive this infilling of the Holy Spirit.

Now, rather than one (Jesus) operating in this anointing, it would be a mighty army of Spirit filled fire baptized believers operating through the authority of His (Jesus) name and performing even greater works.

Jesus was giving His disciples a mandate for the miraculous.

In fact, God never intended for Spirit filled living to be anything less than supernatural. The true church is a supernatural church. And in this church the Super is natural!

This is the very reason that The Holy Spirit was sent!

It is time for the body of Christ to embrace miracle ministry.

This is why I expect miracles!

Wherever Jesus went, He made a business out of putting the devil out of business and everywhere He sent his followers, He expected them to do the same.

"And as ye go, preach, saying, The kingdom of heaven is at hand.Heal the sick, cleanse the lepers, raise the dead, cast out devils: freely ye have received, freely give."
(Matthew 10:7,8)

So why then have we become so content to settle for anything less than what God intended? I have become so tired of church as usual.

Scripted, 45 minute to 60 minutes services. No anointing. No passion. No moving of The Holy Ghost. No salvation. No deliverance. No miracles.
This is not the Kingdom of God.

And for that matter, I am tired of secret service Christians. Folk who hide out in church on Sunday but don't ever share the glorious light of Christ with anyone Monday through Saturday.

The very reason Jesus gave us the Holy Spirit was not to fill a padded pew on Sunday but to walk in power throughout the week.

"And he said unto them, Go ye into all the world, and preach the gospel to every creature."
(Mark 16:15)

You have not been anointed to 'come' to church, you've been anointed to 'Go' into the world. Stop praying for a greater anointing and begin using the one you already have. Get up and go!

Chapter 2
Endued With Power

"And, behold, I send the promise of my Father upon you: but tarry ye in the city of Jerusalem, until ye be endued with power from on high."
(Luke 24:49)

Jesus making this statement, commanded His disciples to wait for the Holy Spirit, the precious promise of the Father. They were forbidden to do a thing until they had received this promised pentecostal power. They had been given their marching orders; *'To go into all the world and reach the gospel to every creature'*

They had been mandated to replicate the ministry of Christ Himself and to do so with signs following but in order to do this, they would have to be baptized in the Holy Ghost. They would need the very same power of God coursing through their veins.

"And, being assembled together with them, commanded them that they should not depart from Jerusalem, but wait for the promise of the Father, which, saith he, ye have heard of me. For John truly baptized with water; but ye shall be baptized with the Holy Ghost not many days hence." (Acts 1:4,5)

It was so important to Jesus, that His instructions were clear....Don't go anywhere until you have be baptized in the Holy Ghost! Don't do anything until you have been endued with power.

It was the very breath of God that breathed into the nostrils of Adam and man became a living soul. And it was the breath of God that blew into that house where the disciples were gathered on Pentecost in Acts chapter 2 and with that very breath the church was birthed to life in power.

So if it took the breath and power of The Holy Spirit to bring life to man and breathe life into the early church, what makes us think we can do anything without Him?

Jesus didn't just die and rise again on the third day to give you salvation and eternal life. He did it to make you a habitation (a dwelling place, a tabernacle, a house) where the very glory of God resides.

> *"In whom ye also are builded together for an habitation of God through the Spirit." (Ephesians 2:22)*

There is a distinct and separate experience subsequent to salvation that God desires and intends for all believers.
It is called *'The Baptism in the Holy Spirit'*.

In the early church this was an accepted fact, they knew that in order fulfill the divine mandate of God they would need to be endued with power from on high.

"The baptism in the Holy Ghost will do more for you than the phone booth did for Clark Kent" Dr. Rod Parsley

This precious infilling of the Spirit of God promised to all believers who ask for it will change your life. It will enhance your prayer life. It will make you sensitive to the voice of God. It will make you acutely aware of the deep holiness and very presence of God. It will energize your praise and invigorate your worship. It will activate and begin to allow the manifestation of the Holy Spirit through the gifts of the Spirit to operate through you. (I'll get into more of that later in the book)

Jesus said you would receive *power* after that the Holy Ghost has come upon you. In the greek, the word translated power is (dunamis) it literally means miracle working explosive power. Its the same root word we get dynamite from.

When you are baptized with the Holy Spirit and full of Him you have tangible spiritual dynamite coursing through your body. Spiritual dynamite to detonate sickness when you pray.

Power to drive out demons.

Dunamis power to live a life that causes Hell itself to tremble in your presence. Power to live and even if necessary die for Christ.

This power will fill you with holy boldness and allow you to stand against all odds and preach the gospel through both word and deed. It is power to be a witness.

Once your filled with the Holy Spirit you will live a compelled life that makes sharing your faith almost automatic.

Sadly many today are wondering around aimlessly in their Christian life devoid of this power and void of this precious infilling.

"I consider that the chief dangers which confront the coming century will be religion without the Holy Ghost; Christianity without Christ; forgiveness without repentance; salvation without regeneration; politics without God; and Heaven without Hell."
William Booth

Society stumbles struggling for a solution to ease its pain. With every stick of a drug addicts needle, with every trick turned by a prostitute, with every callous act of anger, with every slap of an abusive husband, with every extra dollar earned to purchase happiness. Society searches for a solution to calm its screaming conscience. Yet a permanent fix evades them.

Meanwhile the Church has been rocked to sleep in the lap of Delilah. For too long they have believed the liberal theologians that claim the God of the Bible has long ago retired himself with the death of the early Apostles. For too long have Christians lived with sickness racking their bodies, and addictions plaguing their lives.
Supposedly 'born again' believers are flooding the divorce courts rending families in two.

Where is this God of the Bible you ask?
Where have Paul's handkerchiefs and aprons gone?
Where has Peter's shadow gone?
Where have the 3,000 conversions in one day gone?
Where has holiness in the church gone?

Even in the midst of these dark times I have news for you my friend; God still has a remnant of people.

God has a people who long for a return to Pentecostal Power in the church. They long for the presence of the Holy Spirit in their Church services once again.

Their heart cries out for a intimate relationship with their Redeemer.

What the Church needs is not ecumenical reform, its not another program or another seeker friendly function.

What the Church needs is an old fashioned down pour of Holy Ghost power.

What they need is the power of the Holy Ghost to baptize them in fire.

What you need is the Holy Ghost!!

Jesus declared: *"And ye shall receive power after that the Holy Ghost is come upon you: and ye shall be witnesses unto me.." (Acts 1:8)*
He said they would receive 'Power' after that the Holy Ghost has come upon them.

I'm not talking about some little just getting by power.

I'm not talking about some little goose bump experience.

I'm talking about 'POWER' that will wreck your life.....wreck your city....wreck your home and wreck your world!

Power over devils.. Power over depravity.. Power over diseases..

I'm talking about a blind eye opening power...
Wheel chair emptying power...
Miracle working power...

I'm talking about power to live in holiness..

I'm talking about the Holy Ghost of God coming to dwell and take up residence inside you.

I'm talking about the same God who walked on the water.
The same Jesus who set the Gadarene free.
The same God who spoke to the waters and said come this far and no farther.
The same God who raised Lazarus from the dead.
This same God who parted the Red Sea, He wants to make us His habitation through His Spirit living and dwelling in us.

Jesus said His disciples would receive power to be His witnesses. The Greek word for witnesses in this place of scripture is the word 'Martus'. This is the same word we get the English word martyr from.

Jesus declares the disciples would receive power to be witnesses. This word 'witnesses' means 'One who is a spectator of something'

That word means to give evidence of the resurrection of Jesus. What Jesus told them was that they would receive power to give 'evidence' of His resurrection.
I'm talking about resurrection power!
That same Spirit that raised up Christ from the dead wants to dwell in you.

God has ordained the fire baptized church of Jesus Christ to be the answer for a destitute world. I have come to announce to the world that I have the cure to what ails America!

Announcing, that there is healing for your body.

There is deliverance from the snare of drug addiction.

There is a cure for the ravaging disease of AIDS.

There is a cure for cancer, and that cure is the power of the Holy Ghost!

God designed His church to be the hospital for a dying world. It's time to stop outsourcing what Jesus commanded us to cast out. Stop referring out what Jesus commanded us to heal.

God longs for His church to cry out for a fresh outpouring of this Holy Ghost power. He longs for a people who will take this power into their workplaces, into the hospitals, into the markets, into the devils back yard and announce with Resurrection Power... JESUS LIVES!!

This experience with God called the Baptism in the Holy Ghost is intended for all believers. God wants to set you on fire for Him.

Right now where ever you are, throw up your hands and declare; "Father..In the Name of Jesus Christ, baptize me fresh with the Holy Ghost. Fill me with your mighty Spirit and set me on fire. Saturate me with power to give evidence of the resurrection of Jesus Christ. Make me a firebrand of revival!!"

As you yield yourself to the Spirit of God and are baptized in the Holy Ghost you will begin to feel an unknown language and tongue begin to well up on the inside of you, often while your praising God aloud.

Speaking with 'tongues' is the initial evidence of being baptized in the Holy Spirit. As you begin to feel this happening let that beautiful language begin to flow out of your mouth. It may begin just as one syllable or an unknown language but as you begin to speak those words out and allow the Holy Spirit to speak through you. Eventually it will become stronger and more intense.

Praying regularly and frequently in the 'Spirit' or as is often referred to in 'tongues' is the key to walking in the Spirit and operating in the power of God.

And they were all filled with the Holy Ghost, and began to speak with other tongues, as the Spirit gave them utterance. (Acts 2:4)

And when Paul had laid his hands upon them, the Holy Ghost came on them; and they spake with tongues, and prophesied. (Acts 19:6)

But ye, beloved, building up yourselves on your most holy faith, praying in the Holy Ghost. (Jude 1:20)

Chapter 3
The Kingdom of God

"The purpose of a spirit filled life is to demonstrate the supernatural power of our Living God so that the unsaved multitudes will abandon their dead gods to call upon the name of The Lord and be delivered" *T.L. Osborn*

"And as ye go, preach, saying, The kingdom of heaven is at hand. Heal the sick, cleanse the lepers, raise the dead, cast out devils: freely ye have received, freely give." (Matthew 10:7,8)

Jesus had one message. He preached the Kingdom of God. Wherever Jesus went He announced the arrival of the Kingdom. Wherever Jesus went darkness fled. Sickness vanished and dead men were raised to life again. Wherever Jesus went, His Kingdom invaded enemy held territory and vanquished darkness wherever it could be found.

This is the same message our Lord instructed His disciples to preach. He said when you go, announce…"The Kingdom of Heaven is at hand…"

What exactly does that mean?

It means that the Kingdom....(The dominion of the King) has come within your reach.

It means that, whatever you've heretofore been under the dominion of, is now about to come under subjection to the King of Glory.

The message of the Kingdom is the message of the King.

This is the message God called His disciples to carry wherever they went.

"Then he called his twelve disciples together, and gave them power and authority over all devils, and to cure diseases. "And he sent them to preach the kingdom of God, and to heal the sick." (Luke 9:1,2)

This is the same message Paul preached;
"And he went into the synagogue, and spake boldly for the space of three months, disputing and persuading the things concerning the kingdom of God" (Acts 19:8)

"Preaching the kingdom of God, and teaching those things which concern the Lord Jesus Christ" (Acts 28:31)

Whenever this message of the Kingdom (The dominion of The King) was preached it was then subsequently evidenced by demonstration. Jesus did not simply say only preach the Kingdom. He said demonstrate it!
Heal the sick.
Cast out devils.
Raise the dead.
Freely you have received now freely give.

This is the very purpose of the infilling of the Holy Ghost. You have been filled to be poured out. Freely you have received now freely give!

Paul himself said...
"For the kingdom of God is not in word, but in power." (1Cor 4:20)

The very thing that separates the message of the gospel (the Kingdom) from all other religious dogma is the power of God. Without the tangible power of Holy Spirit at work, the message of the Kingdom would be no different than any other philosophy or self help pablum. The message of the Kingdom is a supernatural message from a supernatural King.
It is a message of dominion.
It is a message of power.
It is a message that imposes itself in conquest over every form of satanic resistance
It is a message of revival.
It is a message of healing.
It is a message of deliverance.

It is a message of victory.
It is a message of redemption.
It is a message of love.
It is a message of forgiveness.
It is a message of life.

It is the message of The King (Jesus) and His dominion (His Kingdom)
You have been called to not only carry this message, but impose and implement it wherever you go.

This is a message built on *'greater works'*.

This is a supernatural message with a supernatural mandate.
Miracles, signs and wonders should follow the preaching of the Kingdom.

"These signs shall follow them that believe..." (Mark 16:17,18)

Sign #1 They cast out devils
Unfortunately that may disqualify 90% of so called Christians

Deliverance from demon power has and always will be the initial sign of the Kingdom of God arriving. Wherever Jesus shows up darkness will always flee.
It's time that the church throw out their psychology books and get their faces back into the Bible.

It's time to call it what it is.

It's time to stop trying to counsel out what Good commanded us to cast out.

Sign #2 They speak with new tongues
Holy Ghost tongue talking is the second sign of the Kingdom. The key to supernatural living and the miracle working power of God is tied to your ability to pray in the Spirit.

Paul understood this when he said..
"I thank my God, I speak with tongues more than ye all:" (1 Cor 14:18)

John G Lake, a true general of the faith and a man who walked in a supernatural measure of the power of God, he himself said "Tongues have been the making of my ministry"

If you desire to really walk in the power of God and see the supernatural explode in your personal life.
Pray in tongues and do it daily without ceasing!

Sign #3 They lay hands on the sick and they recover
Healing is 3rd sign of the Kingdom of God showing up.
Everywhere in scripture that you find the Kingdom of God being preached, you will also find the sick being healed. Without exception!

The is the message of the Kingdom. This is the message you are commissioned to carry. The message of the dominion of Jesus.

We have been given supernatural power of attorney to use His name (the name of Jesus) and proclaim Him dominion everywhere we go.

Therefore, wherever you go, He goes.
Greater is He that is in you than he that is in the world and you are the temple of the Holy Spirit who dwells in you. (1 John 4:4; 1 Cor 16:19)

We have been entrusted with this most sacred message and it is the will of God that we be conduits of His mighty power. Vessels of revival wherever we go.
This is the very crux of the Kingdom of God.

It's past time to get out of the confines of our comfort zones and begin to carry the dominion of The King into recesses of society. It's time to reach one hand into the gutter and the other up into glory and pull the two together.

Walk into that crack infested neighborhood and announce.. "The Kingdom of God is at hand!"

Walk into that critical care ward and announce..."The Kingdom of God is at hand!"

Walk into that board room...

Walk into that wayward teenagers bedroom...

Walk into your home....
Walk into your church...

Point your finger under the nose of the devil and tell him enough is enough!

Announce to him, his time is up; The Kingdom of God is here and you are evicting him in the name of Jesus!

"the kingdom of heaven suffereth violence, and the violent take it by force." (Matthew 11:12)

It is time for war!

You have been fashioned for the fight and destined for the victory.
You have been mandated to walk in the supernatural power of God and carry the message of the King.
It's time that you start walking in it today.

The Kingdom of God does not have to ask the mayor for permission.

It does not have to ask the city council for permission.

It does not have to ask the deacon board.

It is not interested in making friends and influencing people.
It does not have need to be counted with the ecumenical boys club and social clubs of its day.

The Kingdom imposes itself!

It is an invading force!

Chapter 4
The Gifts of The Holy Spirit

"Wherever the Holy Ghost has right of way, the gifts of the Spirit will be in manifestation; and where these gifts are never in manifestation, I question whether He is present"
Smith Wigglesworth

"Now concerning spiritual gifts, brethren, I would not have you ignorant."
(1 Corinthians 12:1)

What a statement made by the Apostle Paul!
Sadly today, many in the body of Christ are just as confused today concerning the 9 gifts of the Holy Spirit.
These gifts are as listed in 1 Corinthians 12.
1. The word of wisdom
2. The word of knowledge
3. The gift of faith
4. Gifts of healing
5. The working of miracles
6. The gift of prophecy
7. The discerning of spirits
8. The gift of tongues
9. The gift of interpretation of tongues

These gifts of the Holy Spirit are the manifestation of Jehovah's mighty power in the earth.

They are the very tools and weapons that God has equipped the Spirit filled church with to confront the works of darkness.

The devil's success is dependent upon ignorance. When you understand how to stir and walk in these gifts you will have power and authority over the enemy in every area.

These are the same gifts that Jesus operated in during His earthly ministry.
They are the same gifts that the early church operated in during the book of Acts and they are the very same gifts the modern church is mandated to operate in today.
These gifts are what enabled dead men to be raised back to life again.
They are what enabled the sick to be healed.
They are what enabled demonic schemes to be uncovered and evil spirits driven out.
They are what enabled men of God to prophesy with the accuracy of Heaven.
They are what enabled the secrets of men's hearts to be revealed and laid bare before Jesus Christ.

Just as Paul wrote, *'I would not have you ignorant'*. It is imperative that the church not be ignorant concerning these gifts.

Unfortunately, so many Pastors and church leaders today confuse these 'spiritual gifts' with psychological testing and talents.

It doesn't matter what kind of name is hanging on your church sign out front. We've got some names so long on many of these that we would need to build extensions just to hold them up.

I don't care if you call yourself 'pentecostal', 'charismatic','full-gospel' or even the 'The first church of the assemblies of God of the pentecostal holiness fire baptized charismatic remnant'. If when I get on the inside, its void of power and there aren't any gifts of the Spirit in operation...
If when I get inside and nobody is getting set free...
If they are coming in sick and leaving sick...
If they are coming in lost and leaving lost...
Don't tell me you're Spirit filled.
You're not Spirit filled, you're spirit frilled!

As I will break down through the next few chapters. The gifts of the Holy Spirit have absolutely 'zero' to do with human talents and everything to do with the power of God flowing through his church.

If we are going to walk in a lifestyle of the supernatural.

If you are ever going to walk in the power of God and operate in your mandate for supernatural living.

You are then going to have to learn to operate in and the flow in the gifts of the Spirit.

For too long so called pentecostal churches have claimed to be 'Spirit filled' but are sadly void of any operation of the Holy Ghost other than an occasional 'tongue'. I like to remind my pentecostal brethren that there are 9 gifts of the Holy Ghost and not just 2.

Our services and churches should see regular and frequent operation of all 9 giftings. If you find yourself attending a church where the gifts of the Holy Spirit are not in operation on a regular and daily basis, regardless of the sign hanging up outside...you are NOT in the Spirit filled church.

One of the greatest lies ever perpetrated on the body of Christ is the lie of cessationism. It is this demonically inspired teaching that teaches the gifts of the Spirit and the miracle working power of God ceased to operate any longer in the church once the last of original disciples and the Apostle Paul died.

There is no scriptural basis for this belief and this teaching is completely contrary to the very nature of God.

> *"Jesus Christ the same yesterday, and to day, and for ever. Be not carried about with divers and strange doctrines."* (Hebrews 13:8,9)

Here scripture plainly tells us not to fall for these kinds of strange doctrines (such as cessationism) because Jesus Christ is the same today, yesterday and tomorrow. He does not change!

His mighty power of yesterday is just the same today as it was yesterday and it will be just as available to us tomorrow as it was today.

> *"I was fully convinced of what I had long suspected, That the Montanists, in the second and third centuries, were real, scriptural Christians; and, that the grand reason why the miraculous gifts were so soon withdrawn, was not only that faith and holiness were well nigh lost; but that dry, formal, orthodox men began even then to ridicule whatever gifts they had not themselves, and to decry them all as either madness or imposture."* John Wesley, 1750

Often as had been observed by the great preacher John Wesley, much of the opposition to the gifts and flowing of the Holy Spirit came from the religious elite. As many in these man made places of ecclesiastical authority began to observe others flowing in the power of God, rather than embrace it, they allowed jealousy to set in and persecuted the move of God through the manifestation of a religious spirit.

A few years ago while ministering in Haiti, I was with a colleague and mentor in the faith, Rev. Max Manning. We were discussing the lives of many of the great Generals of the healing ministry that he served personally along side in the 'Voice of Healing' days and so I asked him;
"Brother, what so separated those men like Branham, DuPlessis, Lindsay, Allen and may others you labored with in those days from the preachers of today?"

Without hesitation Rev. Manning turned towards me and replied..

"Without exception Chad, everyone of those men were given to a life of extended periods of fasting. It was during those extended periods of total fasting they would encounter God and never be the same"

He then turned back towards me and added..

"And holiness, they preached holiness...you must hate sin".

What we have to understand, is that we have a Kingdom mandate to walk in this very same supernatural Holy Ghost power but it will not come without paying a price.

Salvation is free but the anointing will cost you.

You have got to pay the price of total consecration to the call of God and to the Lord Jesus Himself.

Will you be serious to answer the call?

Will you be serious to crucify your desires and be consumed with His desires?

"I beseech you therefore, brethren, by the mercies of God, that ye present your bodies a living sacrifice, holy, acceptable unto God, which is your reasonable service."
(Romans 12:1)

There seems to be a frenzy now in the body of Christ to quote the great generals of the past. It seems everyone wants to talk about Smith Wigglesworth, John G Lake, Lester Sumrall or many others.
But if you really want to do what the 'old timers' did, you've got to do what they did.

And what they did, was live holy.
What they did, was eschew the world.

What they did was fast. (I'm not talking about these christian diets that are so popular today) I'm talking about a real extended period of fasting... 3-5-10-15 days or more without any food. No protein shakes...No social media...No television...nothing but the word of God and prayer.

These men got into a prayer closet and were determined to not come out until they were transformed by the very presence of God. These men understood that a world depended on their ability to carry the very glory of God and they would not be satisfied until they became conduits of Holy Ghost power.

Chapter 5
Revelation Gifts

Three gifts of the Holy Spirit listed in 1 Corinthians chapter 12 are often referred to as 'revelation gifts'. In this chapter I will take some time and discuss these operations.

As with all 9 of the gifts of the Spirit, it is important to always remember that Holy Spirit Himself gives these gifts and that they are given with the express purpose and design to benefit and administer the Kingdom of God to the individual in need.

"But the manifestation of the Spirit is given to every man to profit withal" (1 Corinthians 12:7)

The revelation gifts:

1. **Word of Wisdom:** This is the manifestation of Holy Spirit providing supernatural wisdom and revelation through His word during various critical situations. It may be a divine prompting of the Holy Ghost to operate in a level of wisdom to defeat a demonic assignment. Often operating in this gifting can determine life or death situations. This gift often precedes an important decision where it is imperative that you operate solely in the mind of Christ. Understand, that this is not a gift of wisdom, but rather a word of

wisdom. God doesn't gives you the whole picture but a fragment of revelation. This is for a specific need at a specific time.

"The gift of the word of wisdom is a supernatural revelation of divine purposes of God" Lester Sumrall

2. **Word of Knowledge:** This gift also like wisdom, operates as a fragment. A specific word for a specific need. The word of knowledge is a supernatural download of facts known only by the Holy Spirit that could have only been revealed by Him. For example when in operation it may reveal a hidden condition or circumstance.
Often when I function in this gifting, God will reveal to me knowledge about a medical condition in a person that I couldn't have possibly known on my own. This can also include supernatural knowledge revealing an event in the past concerning a person that only God could know.

When this gift is in operation often it is the revelation of knowledge that is brought to the forefront which precedes God's moving to heal and or intervene in a situation.
This specific operation of knowledge will also frequently manifest in conjunction with the gifts of healing, miracles and discernment of spirits.

Sometimes when I am operating in this specific manifestation of the Spirit it may only come as a single 'word' revealed to my spirit. Other times it may be a visual image that I will see over the individual. Like most of the gifts of the spirit, as you step out in faith and begin to operate in it, it will begin to flow one right after the other.

The word of knowledge will connect you to the heart of God in a real way. Often when you are praying for an individual in need, you may get a recurring theme, word, or image that comes to your mind. Many times, I will also feel a specific pain in certain locations of my body that correspond with an individual in need inside the room. When I was new to operating in this gift, I would often feel these unusual pains while preaching in various parts of my body. At first I was confused, I thought that something perhaps was wrong with myself physically.
Suddenly, I was quickened by The Spirit of the Lord, I stopped and announced.
"I am having this unusual pain in my side and I believe God is revealing someones pain to me in this very room.."

Almost immediately an individual came forward and was instantly healed by the power of God.

When this happens it is often God attempting to reveal a word of knowledge to you concerning an individual.
I would encourage you to step out in faith and begin to speak those specific things as you pray or speak with the individual.

You will be amazed at the accuracy as you learn to develop this gift and yield to the Holy Spirit. This sudden revelation of the hidden things and situations revealed to you will open the door for the heart of God to be manifest toward those in need and point them toward The Lord Jesus Christ.

The word of knowledge is supernatural revelation given by the mind of God concerning people, places, or things in present or past.

3. **Discerning of spirits**: This gift is so sorely needed today. It is the perceiving of the source of a particular person, thing or manifestation.

This gift will reveal hidden demonic motives behind individuals and circumstances. It will often determine the difference between someone operating in the flesh or by an evil spirit.

This gift often will be in frequent operation during deliverance ministry. Many times, I will operate in this gift as I stand in front of an individual. While this is in operation, I will literally feel the specific manifestation, thoughts and presence of the particular spirit.

The word to discern means to perceive by seeing or hearing. So by that definition, we understand that this operation allows us to literally see and hear into the spirit realm.

The discerning of spirits is not psychological insight. This is not the power to discern faults in others. This gifting operates not to uncover human failures but to uncover the spirit behind the individual. Whether is it satanic in nature or not.
So many today masquerade this gift as a license to criticize. The gift of the discernment of spirits has everything to do with identifying the spirit realm at work and nothing to do with the agenda of men.

Chapter 6

Vocal Gifts

The next three supernatural gifts of the Holy Spirit that I want to address are what are known as the 'Vocal Gifts'. These three powerful gifts are the literal mouth piece of the Spirit of God.

Often these three gifts work in operation together. 'Different kinds of tongues. Interpretation of tongues and the gift of prophecy'

1. **Tongues:** The gift of 'different' tongues listed here in 1 Corinthians 12:10 is distinct and separate from the tongues received initially from the Baptism in the Holy Ghost. All believers who are baptized in the Holy Spirit will speak with unknown tongues as the Spirit of God gives utterance. (Acts 2:4) The tongues received during and through the Spirit baptism are for personal and private use. This is often referred to as your 'prayer' language.

    As you pray in these unknown tongues you will begin to edify and strengthen your spirit man.

    "But ye, beloved, building up yourselves on your most holy faith, praying in the Holy Ghost" (Jude 20) When you pray in tongues, it is not you that prays but the Holy Spirit who prays through you. When your human mind doesn't know what to pray the Holy Spirit begins to pray through you.

"Likewise the Spirit also helpeth our infirmities: for we know not what we should pray for as we ought: but the Spirit itself maketh intercession for us with groanings which cannot be uttered. And he that searcheth the hearts knoweth what is the mind of the Spirit, because he maketh intercession for the saints according to the will of God." (Romans 8:27,28)

I wanted to differentiate between these two types of tongues. The *'gift of divers or different tongues'* listed here in (1Corinthians 12) is the ability to speak spontaneously by the Spirit of God.

This is used often during corporate worship when the Holy Spirit desires to speak to the corporate body or times to a specific individual. It can be an either an unknown tongue or even a tongue spoken in a language not known by the speaker.

As the individual allows this utterance to come forth it will be subsequently followed up by the interpretation of the tongue given through a spirit filled believer who flows in the gift of interpretation.

2. Interpretation of Tongues: Many times as the public utterance of tongues go forward there will be another individual who operates in the gift of interpretation. This gift will interpret the message given in tongues.
While many times it may be a separate individual who will flow in this gift, other times the person giving the message in tongues may interpret it if they flow in the gift of interpretation. This utterance of interpretation will be audible for those around to hear and be edified by it.

This gift is dependent on the gift of tongues to operate and will flow together with it.

3. The gift of Prophecy: "Wherefore tongues are for a sign, not to them that believe, but to them that believe not: but prophesying *serveth* not for them that believe not, but for them which believe" (1 Corinthians 14:22)

Prophecy is a supernatural utterance in a 'known' tongue. This prophetic gift will exhort, comfort and encourage. This gift will bring forth the mind of God into vocal form. Anything spoken through this prophetic gift must line up with the word of God and be judged by the scriptures.
When an individual operates in this gift they are forth-telling not foretelling.

Although an individual operates in the 'gift of prophecy' it does not mean that they are operating in the five fold gift of 'prophet'.

There is a distinction between the two.

It is the office of the prophet that will often foretell, correct and rebuke.
This is different from the specific gift of prophecy in that this gift will exhort and draw one towards Jesus.

"But he that prophesieth speaketh unto men to edification, and exhortation, and comfort"
(1 Corinthians 14:3)

The bible actually tells us that we should all earnestly seek this gift.

"Follow after charity, and desire spiritual gifts, but rather that ye may prophesy"
(1 Corinthians 14:1)

"Wherefore, brethren, covet to prophesy, and forbid not to speak with tongues. Let all things be done decently and in order."
(1 Corinthians 14: 39,40)

This is the gift that all spirit filled believers should earnestly pray for. It is this gift that will edify, exhort and comfort one another.

It is vitally important that we do not allow ourselves to despise prophesy or discount its vitality to our spiritual life.
Often many, especially Pastors will foster an atmosphere of 'quenching the spirit' and despising of this prophetic gift due to the fact that this is one of those specific gifts that they themselves cannot control.

"Despise not prophesyings"
(1Thessalonians 5:20)

Prophecy is the vehicle designed by God to carry a message from Him to others. The is the medium upon which the heart of God breaks forth into language.

It is important to note that the simple 'gift of prophecy' is not the ministry of criticism.

While all Spirit filled believers may prophesy- all are not prophets.
One important thing to address here also is that just because something is revealed it may not be proper to released it yet.
We must wait for the release of God to give the word.
A message may be received but the proper unction may not be yet given.

Learn to be sensitive to the leading of the Holy Spirit.

The individual does indeed have the ability to speak or not speak and must be able to exercise self-control. (1 Corinthians 14:3)

As with all of the gifts of the Spirit, everything operates by and through faith. Often we will not have the entire 'picture' prophetically as we prophesy. Learn to flow.

Many times as we step out and begin to prophesy, we will only know a small piece or have an unction.
However, as we begin to release the prophetic and step into faith it will just begin to flow like a faucet.

"For we know in part, and we prophesy in part"
(1 Corinthians 13:9)

Chapter 7
Power Gifts

The gift of faith, gift of healings and the gift of the working of miracles are what are commonly known as 'power gifts'. These three supernatural gifts often work together and are many times in operation simultaneously. Let's take a moment and examine each if these 'power gifts'.

These 3 gifts are the physical manifestation of the power of God upon the earth. It is through these three gifts that the Holy Spirit moves to bring, healing, work miracles and thwart the power of the devil.

1. The Gift of Faith: The word of God tells us that God has dealt to every man 'the measure of faith'. (Romans 12:3)

'The measure of faith', has to do with the ability to believe in Christ for salvation. All men are given this 'measure' or ability of faith and it is completely separate from the 'gift of faith'. The gift of faith has nothing to do with the 'measure of faith which is given to men to believe on Christ.

The supernatural gift of the Holy Spirit known as the 'gift of faith' is a supernatural endowment of faith given for a particular moment, season or task. This is the immediate assurance of the Holy Ghost to act in a specific situation. This 'gift of faith' does not regard the natural laws of physics or even fact. It considers only the truth of God's word to intervene in a specific moment.

This gift of faith is most assuredly present when the gift of the working of miracles is in operation. It takes this kind of supernatural faith to raise the dead and to believe God for creative miracles.

This is special faith which accesses the power of the Holy Spirit to move beyond the ordinary.

The gift of faith is the greatest of the 3 power gifts. It is given to the believer in order to receive miracles whereas the working of miracles is given to the believer to work miracles.

The gift of faith is distinct in that it is passive while the working of miracles is active. The difference is the the gift of special faith passively receives while the gift of miracles actively creates a miracle.

2. The Working of Miracles: This is a supernatural creative act. This power gift is the manifestation of the power of God to annual the laws of science and nature.

It was this gift in operation that enabled Jesus to calm the sea. It was this gift in operation the parted the Red Sea. It was this gift in operation that raises dead men back to life again.

This gift is separate from the gifts of healings in that healing is a work of restoration. Miracles are a creative act.

For example; a deaf ear opening or a blind eye seeing are examples of the gift of healings. They are healings that resulted from the immediate restoration of something that presently existed but was not functioning properly.
The formation of an eye in an eye socket that did not previously exist is an example of the working of miracles.

Creative miracles fall into this category.

I believe that we are on the precipice of a fresh activation of this gift in the body of Christ.

"God anointed Jesus of Nazareth with the Holy Ghost and with power: who went about doing good, and healing all that were oppressed of the devil; for God was with him." (Acts 10:38)

Jesus was anointed to work miracles and then passed the spiritual baton to us, 'His church' as He announced;
"He that believeth on me, the works that I do shall he do also; and greater works than these shall he do; because I go unto my Father. (John 14:12)

Operating in this gift is a part of the supernatural mandate to manifest the Kingdom of God in the earth.

3. The Gift of Healings: This power gift is plural and not singular because it can apply to any area of life both physical or emotional. Often this gift can also come into effect with a gradual healing or immediate healing.

Healing is a restorative gift. It restores what is broken. This can include an innumerable type of healings.
The laying upon of hands upon the sick is primarily how this gift operates but not exclusively.
For example, I have operated in this gift while laying hands on the afflicted as God instantly opened blinded eyes, healed those suffering from HIV and healed those suffering from many other horrendous afflictions.
I have also operated in this gift without laying hands on the individual but flowed in this simply by speaking the word of the Lord and the sick were healed.

I was preaching a crusade in Uganda and a mother and father brought their blind 5 year old boy to the meeting. They were so desperate for a miracle that they traveled 7 hours by foot to reach the crusade grounds.
Determined to receive their boy's healing they came in faith...

As I prayed for that young boy, the Spirit of God came upon me and I prophesied…"In 4 days you will see…"

They took the young boy home and on the fourth night according to the word of the Lord, his eyes immediately popped open.
He could see!

He was healed by the supernatural power of God!

Glory to God!

God wants to use you to operate in these very same 9 gifts of the Holy Spirit. He wants you t one a conduit of His power as you manifest the Kingdom of God everywhere you go.

Chapter 8
Partnering with The Holy Spirit

"If the Holy Spirit was withdrawn from the church today, 95 percent of what we do would go on and no one would know the difference. If the Holy Spirit had been withdrawn from the New Testament church, 95 percent of what they did would stop and everybody would know the difference." *A.W. Tozer*

"And I will pray the Father, and he shall give you another Comforter, that he may abide with you for ever" (John 14:16)

The greek word for *Comforter* is (paraklētos) it literally means to come along side of another, The helper, encourager, and assistant.
The Holy Spirit is that very Comforter.
He is the third person in the Godhead.
The Spirit of God Himself who has been sent to come along side of us.

He has been sent to prop us up when we can no longer stand on our own. He has been sent to encourage us when need encouragement. He has been sent to strengthen us when we cannot do it on our own. He has been sent to assist us in fulfilling the great commission. He has been sent to empower us to work the very works of Jesus.

He is the Holy Spirit, God Himself and without Him we can do nothing, but with Him *ALL THINGS* are possible!

There is no way to possibly even fathom fulfilling the command of Jesus to work greater works unless we be completely yielded and submitted to the Holy Spirit.

He is the one who makes it possible.

Holy Spirit is actively leads, guiding and speaking. It is imperative that we listen and remain sensitive to His voice.

After all, the very 9 gifts of the Spirit are His gifts. They belong to Him and Him alone. As we are submitted to Him, He will manifest Himself through us by their operation in our lives.

We carry the very mandate of heaven upon us. It is the mandate of the supernatural. It is the mandate to manifest the Kingdom of God in the earth. It is a mandate to bring deliverance to the bound. It is the mandate to carry healing to the sick. It is the mandate to destroy the power of the devil. It is the mandate to shake cities, regions and nations with the power of God.

This is a mandate that we must fulfill at all costs.It is one that we must be dedicated to seeing manifested in every area of our lives.

Everywhere we go we are called to exact this mandate in the earth.
Not by our own power or strength, but by the power of the Holy Ghost.

We are called to impose the Kingdom of Jesus in our cities. To imprint our very DNA on the culture around us.

For far too long the church has been operating devoid of Holy Spirit power.
For far to long powerless preachers and petrified churches have banished the moving of the Holy Spirit.

Many have treated the Spirit of God and His operation in our midst as if He is some crazy uncle who shows up on special occasions and therefore must be handcuffed and kept at arms length.

Not too long ago, I had a Pastor tell me that the church down the street from his was recently holding a discipleship class and one of the people attending asked the Associate Pastor teaching the class..

"Why don't we have the Holy Ghost and the gifts in our services, we want the Holy Ghost"

The Pastor responded, "Well.. if you want the Holy Ghost you're gonna have to go to that little church down the street...they got the Holy Ghost over there"

Can you believe this? How sad!!

My friend tells me that this particular 'so called' minister admitted to him that he even refers everyone seeking the Holy Ghost down the street to his church.

My friends response.."Keep on sending them!!!"

Folks I'm not making this stuff up!!!

If you go to a church that puts a muzzle on the Holy Ghost...GET OUT!!!

If you go somewhere that thinks the gifts of the Spirit are only on some psychological test designed to reveal talents and then mislabels them as spiritual gifts...GET OUT!!

Just an FYI, there are 9 gifts of the Holy Spirit not just 2 and if all 9 don't operate where you go..GET OUT!!

If you go somewhere that prays for the sick by saying..."Lord if it be thy will...' -GET OUT!!

If you go somewhere that refers out devil's rather than casting them out...GET OUT!!

If you go somewhere where people no longer get saved....GET OUT!!!

If your services are scripted....GET OUT!!

Flee dead cold religiosity- Flee Ichabod

We need the Holy Spirit and Jesus specifically sent Him to operate along side us and through us. We must have Him!

We must be so desperate for the moving of the Spirit of God that nothing else will satisfy.

We must hunger!

We must thirst!

When you don't know how your gonna make it.

When you don't know how much longer you can hold on.

That is when the Holy Spirit will show up and intervene on your behalf.

I often have found myself asking the same question as did Mary...

"How shall this be?.."

And instantly the Spirit of God responded, "The Holy Ghost shall come upon thee and the power of the most high shall overshadow thee"

In other words...God's got this and I'm just along for the ride!

> *"Then said Mary unto the angel, How shall this be, seeing I know not a man? And the angel answered and said unto her, The Holy Ghost shall come upon thee, and the power of the Highest shall overshadow thee"* (Luke 1:34,35)

This Kingdom mandate that we carry to go into all the world and shake it with the gospel of Jesus Christ can only be fulfilled when we understand that we are completely and totally dependent on the Holy Spirit.

> *"And they went forth, and preached every where, the Lord working with them, and confirming the word with signs following."* (Mark 16:20)

As they went. Read it again.
Faith begins as you go.
Don't tell me you have faith but you refuse to 'go'.

They went and God showed up. Often, Holy Spirit will not show up until you first 'go'.

Do you want God to move in your life?
Then learn to step out in faith and 'go'.

The bible here shows us that it was the Lord who was working *'with'* them. The paraklētos, the Holy Spirit Himself was working along side them.
And as they went and preached, it was the Lord who confirmed His word with signs, wonders and miracles following.

The ministry of the Holy Ghost is a supernatural ministry. When we learn to partner with Him (Holy Spirit) on a daily basis we will then begin to walk in the supernatural.

Chapter 9

Walking in the Supernatural

"We should never overlook the power of the anointing God has for us. Before I attempt to do anything for God, I cry out in prayer for His anointing." *Dr. Oral Roberts*

"You can never cross the ocean until you have the courage to loose sight of the shore"
Christopher Columbus

In every area of your life. You can access the supernatural power of God. From the very beginning, mankind was created to walk in fellowship with God. That was the original plan of God before sin entered this planet. This is what Jesus came to restore. True fellowship with The Father.

You were originally created a spirit being first. Mankind has been created as spirit-soul-body. However, the fall of Adam's original sin has reversed that order of priority.

Due to sinful and carnal living, man has been operating with his soul (mind, will, and emotions) in the seat of authority. When we operate from a soulish position in life we make decisions based on emotions and in the confines of the human mind.

The spirit filled believer was never designed to operate this way. We are called to walk by faith and not by sight. We have been designed by the original plan of God to walk in the spirit and therefore not fulfill the desires of the flesh.

> *"This I say then, Walk in the Spirit, and ye shall not fulfil the lust of the flesh. For the flesh lusteth against the Spirit, and the Spirit against the flesh"* (Galatians 5:16,17)

When you constantly allow yourself to be led by what you see, hear and feel, you will find yourself handcuffed to fear unable to break into the blessing of true Spirit filled living.

If you truly want to see the power of God operate in your life, you must be totally submitted to being led by the Holy Spirit. You must be determined to walk by faith and not by sight.

> *"For we walk by faith, not by sight"*
> *(2 Corinthians 5:7)*

Stop governing your life by what you see in the natural realm. Don't be moved by what you see, be moved only by what you believe.

Understand this, that the supernatural realm-the unseen spiritual realm, is even more real than the temporal natural realm you observe and live in every day. In the Kingdom of God, the supernatural should be natural.

"Now faith is the substance of things hoped for, the evidence of things not seen."
(Hebrews 11:1)

Faith is not just a verb, its a noun. Faith is a substance. It is the literal evidence of that which is unseen.

So while walking in, by and of faith we understand that true faith doesn't create. True faith reaches from the natural realm into the unseen realm and accesses what already exists in the heavens.

Unfortunately, so many christians never fully walk in the full potential that Christ provided for them. They live a life trapped by the philosophies of men and bound by a system of fear.

Many times I'm asked after I return from an international crusade. "Why does it seem that more miracles happen in places like Africa.."

The answer to this has nothing to do with geographical boundaries. The power of God is not bound by geopolitical boundaries.
God is only bound by your ability to believe Him.

In America it has become too convenient to not have to trust God.

In Africa they have the 'Great Commission' - In America we have the 'Great Prescription'

If you want to truly access the supernatural power of God. You must learn to hunger for the word of God. Spend time in prayer. Turn everything else off and get in turn with Holy Spirit.

"I want to talk with the utmost frankness and say to you, that tongues have been the making of my ministry. It is that peculiar communication with God when God reveals to my soul the truth I utter to you day by day in the ministry. Many times, I climb out of bed, take my pencil and pad, and jot down the beautiful things of God, the wonderful things of God that He talks out in my spirit and reveals to my heart." John G. Lake

John Lake was one of greatest generals of faith and power to walk in the body of Christ in centuries.
This was a man who operated in the miracle working power of God so strongly that during an outbreak of plague in Africa he held a handful of infected vomit to prove that the virus would die on contact with his hand.
As he held the specimen up before the doctor, the medical professional couldn't believe what he was seeing!

The doctor would record that the very plague did indeed die instantly upon contact with John's body.

The anointing that Brother Lake walked in was directly proportionate to his determination to pray fervently in the Holy Ghost on a daily basis.

When I prepare to preach, as is my custom I usually fast for three days prior to the meetings. However, I make specific effort to pray extendedly in the Holy Spirit. Often for hours during the day I will pray in tongues. This is truly the secret to walking in the power of God.

If you have not been baptized in the Holy Spirit with the evidence of speaking in other tongues, ask Jesus to fill you with the Holy Ghost. This is promised to all believers who will seek it. This is one of the greatest keys to walking in the supernatural.

"And ye shall receive power after that the Holy Ghost is come upon you" (Acts 1:8)

Conclusion

"Beloved, for the sake of a lost and dying world, pay any price, get God's power and set the prisoners free." *John G. Lake*

As one would look around it seems apparent to the eye of the flesh that all hope is lost. With every turn of the television channel, scroll across social media or blog posted- it seems that the world is falling apart. So it appears that darkness has triumphed and all that is left is corruption, disease, death and depravity.

Nothing could be farther from the truth.

We are not of this world and we do not look at things with the eye of the flesh. I look behind what is seen and pierce the veil of the natural realm to what lies just beyond in the supernatural realm. If you would listen to the voice of the Holy Spirit you would both hear and see it as well.

While it may look like its bleak all around, what you actually are seeing in the natural is simply the manifestation of the womb that will birth the greatest move of God ever to kiss this planet.

> *"Arise, shine; for thy light is come, and the glory of the Lord is risen upon thee. For, behold, the darkness shall cover the earth, and gross darkness the people: but the Lord shall arise upon thee, and his glory shall be seen upon thee.And the Gentiles shall come to thy*

light, and kings to the brightness of thy rising." (Isaiah 60:1-3)

I believe that the church today. The 'Ekklesia' the called out ones with the mandate to decree the legislative verdict of Heaven in the earth could not be in a better position.

While darkness seems to abound, it is then and only then that the glory of God is going to be released. With the explosive force of a million atomic devices, the power of God is going to shake this planet and revival is going to reverberate across the land.

Like a mighty army, the church is going to carry the glory of the Most High and reach one hand into the gutter and the other up into glory and pull the two together. This isn't a time to hide under a pew and just wait for Jesus com back. This is the time to *'Arise and Shine'-*

This is the time to walk in the glory of God and be a conduit of revival. You were created to walk in the supernatural- You were created to carry the very presence and power of God.

"In whom ye also are builded together for an habitation of God through the Spirit." (Ephesians 2:20)

You have been sanctified and redeemed by the blood of Jesus so that you could be filled with the Holy Ghost and become a habitation of God. A literal place where the Spirit of God takes up residency.

You carry His presence and His power-

It's time to manifest the Kingdom of God in the earth.

Preach the message of Jesus, manifest the Kingdom of Jesus and live the message of Jesus. There are millions that depend on your ability to preach Jesus and manifest the Kingdom of God. You have been called to walk in the supernatural!

"And as ye go, preach, saying, The kingdom of heaven is at hand. Heal the sick, cleanse the lepers, raise the dead, cast out devils: freely ye have received, freely give" (Matthew 10:7,8)

About The Author

Chad MacDonald carries a powerful apostolic anointing that will change your life. He is the founder of Revival Fire World Ministries, author, international revivalist and prophetic voice.

Chad travels extensively internationally and across America carrying a Kingdom mandate to preach deliverance to the captives and equip the body of Christ.
His meetings are marked with the tangible presence of God and accompanied by powerful signs and wonders. His heart burns to see the fire of revival sweep the globe and a generation transformed by the power of God.

He can also be heard on his weekly radio broadcast 'Voice of Revival' which currently airs on KFGB radio 97.7FM in Topeka, KS.

Through Revival Fire World Ministries, Chad is also active in the pioneering and planting of vibrant Spirit Filled churches in various nations as the Holy Spirit directs. It is through the network of these churches, many of which are in areas under severe threat of extremist persecution that will become conduits of revival and power in their respective regions.

Booking or Contact Information

For bookings or more information contact and follow Chad on social media: @revivalfirewm or on the web: www.miraclerevivalfire.com

P.O. Box 9311
Chattanooga, TN 37412

Additional Resources

Additional Books By The Author

Rise And Be Healed —It is always God's will for you to be healed. God's power is available to heal and deliver today. Learn how you can walk in the miracle working power of God and in victory over sickness and satan.

Casting Out Devils – The first commandment of our Lord concerning the commission of the church was to confront the powers of darkness and cast out demons. The ministry of Christ centered around liberating those held captive by the devil and so also should the ministry of the church equally be centered around such. God is restoring the power of deliverance ministry back to the body of Christ and you too can walk in that power today. 'Casting Out Devils' is a powerfully anointed handbook on deliverance ministry.

Prayer That Makes Hell Tremble – Praying people don't faint and fainting people don't pray. The key to standing victorious in the white hot throes of spiritual warfare is a fervent prayer life. Have you ever wondered why some of your prayers seem to go unanswered? 'Prayer That Makes Hell Tremble' is a handbook and guide to engaging with the glory of God. The revelatory truths that Chad MacDonald details in 'Prayer That Makes Hell Tremble' will revolutionize your prayer life and draw you into a deeper relationship with the Holy Spirit as you learn to pray and not faint.

These books and many other resources are available through our ministry store and wherever books are sold:

www.miraclerevivalfire.com